The Garbage Can Experiment

A Collection of Poetry and Spoken Word

Robert M. Brandy
and other voices from the inside

BOLDFACE BOOKS

Edited by Monica Fuhrmann
Design by Hanh Le

Dedicated to Dyveonne, J'Vionne, Xzavier, and Jada.
Without struggle there is no progress and through you
all I have found meaning in the midst of my suffering.

I am forever indebted to my brothers who've poured
their hearts and souls onto these empty pages bringing
forth life, healing and hope. Without you there is no us...
U.N.I.T.Y.

The degree of civilization in a society can
be judged by entering its prisons.

DOSTOYEVSKY

The negro came for the white man for a
roof or for $5 or for a letter to the judge;
the white man came to the negro for love.
But he was not often able to give what he
came seeking. The price was too high; he
had too much to lose. And the Negro knew
this too. When one knows this about a man,
it is impossible for one to hate him, but
unless he becomes a man—becomes equal—
it is also impossible for one to love him.

JAMES BALDWIN

Contents

The Power 38

Only a Cage 64

Introduction:
The Garbage Can Experiment

Look at you, Black man, you're vulnerable. You walk around as if you have no worries, no direction; you're lost. I have a place for you. A place where your children, family, and friends will forget about your very existence. It's all a part of my design and plan for you. You won't need any transportation for this ride you're about to take. Don't worry, I'll pick you up on my bus and I will provide your basic necessities: food, clothing, and shelter. All free of charge.

I'm accepting all minorities so this includes you too my brown Latino brothers. There's enough room for you here too. Your dreams can also be put on a respirator. Along with a little division, I will break down your 33 vertebrates and dismember any solidarity you have left in your very soul.

Don't worry my poor White brothers, I have this saying I go by I'm sure you've heard of it before. It's called "No Child Left Behind." You too are welcome aboard this bus, we have plenty of room. We are color blind here, the only color we recognize is Green.

Once you all get to your new home we will go over some rules. I want my Black brothers – we are brothers, aren't we? – I want you to destroy one another; never unite. I want you to rob and fight one another even to the death. Go on ahead and form your gangs, it's all right, and that way you'll never unite. Promise me you'll never read any books about W.E.B. DuBois, Nelson Mandela, Marcus Garvey, or any prominent black leaders. We will teach you everything you need to know about yourself. You don't need to search for yourself, for who you are. You don't have time for that. Just keep reading your Triple Crown books, XXL's and playing cards and dominoes. We don't want you reading any of those Black Enterprises, or anything about your culture and history; those things are all poison and will be considered contraband.

If you can behave yourself and be a good boy then I will give you a little treat. I'll let you shop at my store once a week. Just have your family make the money orders out in your name, but we can keep the money in my bank. So, it's just like it's the both of ours. You trust me, don't you? Don't I treat you right? I put a roof over your head, clothes on your back, and food in your stomach. I do my best. I even give you $16 a month just for your pocket money. Now don't you be ungrateful, I only physically put my hands on you because I love you.

It's not my fault your family doesn't get to see you often or that your kids hardly even know you and some of them you never even met. You can't blame me. I had to take you far away from your communities, away from your families, and away from your love. That's the only way I knew you would listen to me. Don't worry, you never have to leave here. I'll never abandon you! You'll always have a place to call your home.

All I ask is that you continue to destroy each other instead of building one another up. Stay divided so you'll never rule the world. And please don't ever reach your highest potential. Realization that you were born to be KINGS!

Love Always,
The Garbage Can Experiment

P.S. Please don't forget to let your children and grandchildren know all about me. I can't wait to meet them.

From
the Dirt

A Portrait of Poverty

Robert M. Brandy

Sugar water, syrup sandwiches, free food place!
Drug dealers, dope fiends, rent was late

Late for school, lights don't work, make ends meet
Product of my environment, get through the week

Succeed in life, be all you can be! Try to survive,
Stuck in debt, addicted to dope, Wanted – dead or alive!

They been stop using whips to beat our flesh
We war with one another, and fight to the death

If you put a face on Poverty,
It would look just like us

Black and Brown people with no one to trust
System is flawed with structural errors

While the rich get rich,
The Poor – nobody cares!

Acknowledge Me

Robert M. Brandy

I'm regulated by the federal government to be at least 10 feet long by
    4 feet wide.
During the hot summer nights, my walls perspire and I hold heat like
    an oven,
Causing a great discomfort for the millions who inhabit my space.
I cause havoc in the winter season, acting as an ice box,
Allowing cold air to circulate freely,
Causing all who occupy my space to reside underneath covers.
My walls are full of neglect due to old age and harsh treatment.
They are institutional white with paint peeling from top to bottom;
Gang graffiti, calendar dates, and bible scriptures litter the walls
These scars have withstood the test of time.
I've been known to use my tight quarters to squeeze my inhabitants,
Confiscating any glimmer of hope they have of leaving me behind.
I am a prison cell; acknowledge me.

RED + BLUE = BLACK

Robert M. Brandy

Masquerade my pain with deep thoughts
That only anger can feel
But who can I blame
See I fall victim to the con game
Thought I was a better thinker
But how shrewd the system be

He had an old soul
Lost in the rhythm of Life
Red was for the Blood
That he swore on his life
He know the way he living ain't right
But Red was the color
That depicted his Life

You see dude had a Ruger or a Larkin
It was Black
And when he squeezed that trigger
It pushed that boy's chest to his back
And when he fell to the ground
We knew he never make it back

He was Black
I guess that's just another fact Cuzz,
The kids looking up to him
But he ain't looking back

He bleed Blue
And when it's war he send Da Crew
And they attack
He did the math

But the answer's wrong
Cause he forgot to subtract

Now Red and Blue look so confused
Cause they both sleeping on a mat
And the sad thing about this story
these Brothers Black

Dope Boy (Spoken Word)

Robert M. Brandy

You a sell ya mom a stone
So you can rock a precious stone
But that chain around ya neck
Won't mean much when yo head gone
But go on, get yo shine on
Them same jewels that you rockin'
Them young goons got they eyes on
Cartiers on his face
But he walk around with blind folds
For his wrist watch
Shorty walked up on 'em with his eyes closed emptied the clip
And dumped his body in a different time zone
I guess that's how it's layin'
When you tryna get ya shine on
Dude wanted my advice
So I threw 'em a gem
Told 'em that that chain around his neck
Was drawing attention to him
He said his life was like steel on bone
A hard grind
He done came up from the bottom
And just wanted to shine
If some jewels compromise your worth
They own you
That record exec who put that chain around ya neck
Don't let 'em own you
Peace!

Yesterday I Cried

Robert M. Brandy

It's not how you start your life but how you end it
We can't change the past
but can relive it,
So be careful my Love
Don't you come off ya pivot,
Wipe your tears on my cheek, ask the Lord for forgiveness,
For you are the definition of what strength is

Yesterday I cried
For a better tomorrow
If I could erase that day I'd start over tomorrow
Where my sons and my daughter
Would be hidden from sorrow
Yesterday I cried
For a better tomorrow

Yesterday I cried
But no tears were coming out
I saw an image of a woman's face and it was full of doubt,
I tried so hard to recognize the face but couldn't make it out,
She seemed to be going through some things
So I offered to help her out and when she smiled
I recognized her face
As tears came streaming out
Yesterday I Cried!

You Should Have Been There

Robert M. Brandy

On the first day of school, I wanted you to meet my teachers
But you were nowhere to be found
You should have been there
When mommy struggled to keep food in my stomach
    and clothes on my back,
You could have helped

You should have been there
Where were you at after all those years
How can you make it up to me after all those tears
Why should I trust you?
So, you can let me down
You should have been there

It's too late now.

My First Love

Andre Winters

At first glance I remember dreaming about the first chance
For us to be intimate
Sweet long kisses a nice grip full, both fists
Oh, now I could love her, place nothing above her
Everybody liked her, but she chose me
Yea, she became my first
I was deeply attracted to her blackness
Black like the night
Black in the light a sight so exquisitely explicit
A love I never had to be with
Or lay up and cuddle with was one thing "Dre" never did
You would of thought I knew better
But who really knows better?
She was gorgeously stunning while strikingly charming
This made her appealing to me
See, what it was; she knocked me out the gate
She was good with her ability to allure and captivate, caress my heart
Fondle my mind with enticing lies
So mesmerizing instantly she became the apple of my eyes
And I loved everything about her
Her panoramic views, her talk
From the beginning of knowledge, I was bought and locked in like livestock
With feelings growing fond she made other girls jealous of our bond
Sold for the gold like glitter
Ignoring what was shown
Forgetting what was told
I found my way to her head and laid in it
Feeling manipulated as I fingered her every angle, thinking to myself who
    gaming who?
As she guided me in with her warm embrace and I hugged and kissed her
    every crevice, curve, and corner
I thought some more on it and what I came up with was

This chick, this broad, the love of my life
The one I too eagerly called my wife, was two-timing on me with my dad
Uncles, brothers, cousins and friends
And a host of others
I'm pretty sure you know her too
She broke my virginity
Took my innocence
Fooled me with a love I thought was heaven sent
That's only a scratch off the surface of deception that's deeply rooted
See this chick robbed and ruined me
She was rude and shrewd like how dudes be
It took me this long to realize that she has no morals, rules nor loyalty
She never loved me
So I know I gotta let her be, but she keep on calling me
What would you do? The Streets will always be my first love

Time + Trust = Love

Robert M. Brandy

Don't want to press too hard
Might scare this one away
Knowing that nothing last forever
I live my life from day to day
I try not to attach my feelings
Because I don't want to get hurt
If love don't cost a dime
Then tell me what is it really worth?

Never mind about love,
I try and leave that word alone
Because the second you say love to someone
They'll leave you all alone

I Can't See Over the Fence

Robert M. Brandy

Man's search for meaning
On a journey searching for self
Tell me if you find Him
Maybe I can help?
It's that Wisdom speaking to Us
But we never want to listen
The same energy that you put out into the world
Is the same that you'll be given
And what is actually living?
Because existing ain't
We should try a little harder
Instead of saying "I can't"
But, what I know is I'm in a fish tank
Surrounded by Hustlers and Legends
Freedom or Heaven?
You gotta choose one
Am I wrong for wanting to hold my son
Seen a patient man waiting when I saw my reflection
They say the blind a lead the blind
Better follow directions
They do a good job of avoiding and never answer the question
But what I know
You in the Free World
And I can't see over the fence

Portrait of Pain

Cecil Johnson

Visualize my life's blood descending as rain,
A product of poverty painting a portrait of pain
As the colors blend, my whole life is distorted
The weight of a burdened heart left unsupported
What happens once the colors of life eventually become one shade
Time merges as night continuously turns to day,
A spectrum of light ultimately turns to gray
How my thoughts reside where dreams and reality mesh,
While my spirit experiences the weakness of flesh
Pain has painted a portrait so vivid and clear,
Though it's hard to recognize with so much darkness in here
The bastard seed has inherited his father's sin,
Leave the door cracked and the snakes will wander in
Through blood and tears my life's portrait is drawn,
An entire existence carved and etched in stone
My pursuit of prosperity produced a permanent stain,
Now all that remains is this portrait of pain.

Dreams

Robert M. Brandy

When dreams and reality mesh, a star is born
But what happens when that dream's deferred?
Will it return again – like the resurrection of Christ
Or like a convict back to prison who's on his third strike,
And if chance favors the prepared mind,
Then why my people got they hands out
Instead of on they damn grind.
And stop begging for change,
When every single day we got young black kids dying for change
Yea, my president is black
But whatever happened to that man's Dream…

She Doesn't Know She's A Queen

Robert M. Brandy

Her face would glow with the countenance of life
Just one more taste and everything will be alright
Well the devil is a lie and speaks not the truth
"I know you better than yourself, I even named you Ruth"

Let's discuss how this addiction first began
Let me guess, it was recreational; it used to be fun?
The same as David killing Goliath with a sling and a rock
Is parallel to the drug dealers who sling on the block

Wake up! Stand up!
Rise from the dirt
Take a good look at yourself and realize your worth
When you put down that glass pipe and stop looking through
    that smoke screen
Only then will you awake to realize you're a Black Queen!

As One

Over the Top

Kevin Short

Until Mass Incarceration is no longer an issue,
Until the likes of our people break the chains of Psychological Slavery
which keeps us under the Spell of Materialism and Poverty,
Until the low-down Separatist feels the Breeze of Equality,
Until my Voice is heard from the Smallest Crack in the Ground,
I'll Drag my Cup across my Bars and make the craziest Sound,
Until We understand the Negative Influences that Target our Youth,
and show them We can obtain Freedom through the Light of our Truth,
Change is a Necessity for tangible Proof,
Entombed and Confined is No more The Excuse,
So, we can Unite Together as One,
Then and only then can We shine bright as the Sun,
Until I've Accomplished a fraction of what Our Leaders have Done,
Even when Our People are in that X state of Mind,
Truth and Freedom Fighters misled by Elders who lost their way in
    the midst of the Grind,
In Depression like Times,
Looking up from a Caged Floor,
While every other Atom races to Victory,
I wait Silent and Patient as I pick at a lock which
Incarcerates the longitudinal bars of My Door,
While humming and Singing Songs of Redemption,
Visions of Critiquing and Masterpiece marvels of my own inventions,
Until the Words of Me burn deep into the Heart,
Not yours but a blueprint for those off the porch into a Genesis of an un-for-
    told start,
Until We see the wave from the Splash we created and its effects on Our
    Community,
Out of the Womb of the Beast we travel as One,
A Unit,
Our U.N.I.T.Y.!

Black Diamond

Robert M. Brandy

Listen to the wind and follow the path of the wise,
The inner voice that's speaking to you is meant to be your guide,
How can man define you when you know who you really are?
Stop acting like you don't deserve it when you really are a star,
Listen to the wind,
Take time to hear the rain,
If life was meant to be enjoyed then why we feeling pain?

Perpetuate Violence

Robert M. Brandy

Nonviolence, nonviolence
We shall not be moved
But how can one be at peace in the middle of a war?
It's justified retribution when we kill each other
When we put our hands on them
We a "bitch" and a "motherfucka"
I'm a black man living in a white man's world
Respect for those who make it without selling their soul
Solidarity to the moms struggling, having to play the father's role
Can't miss something you never had, like freedom and equality
I guess we all still paying for our father's sins
So much pain and animosity all coming from within
Must of been the slave trade
Got us lashing out and killing one another over some damn change
I can only shake my head because I know this shit a damn shame
Perpetuate violence
It's alright with me
As long as you stand for something you can unite with me
Revolutionize your thinking
That's the fight we need
Last call for all soldiers
Come unite with me!

Letter to a Black Boy

Tony Curtis, Jr.

Dear Black Boy,
Black Boy, it's a lot going on
Poverty makin' things hard at home
You probably grew up in a single parent home
Black Boy, be careful of how you move
It's a lot of people praying you lose
Never forget you was convicted in the womb
Black Boy, some people will never see past your skin
In their eyes being black is a deadly sin
One wrong encounter could be the end
Black Boy, you will be called nigger by those who hate you
Nigga by those you love
But your neither ·of the above
Black Boy, you're a King, a Great Man, a work of art
In everything you do you must stay true to your heart
Set no limits on what you want to do
And all your dreams will one day come true
Black Boy, many will have you believe you're not good enough
Some people will tell you you're not smart enough
Some will have you believe you're destined to fail
Even try to convince you that you belong in a cell
Black Boy, you was made in the image of God
What anybody else think pay it no mind
Just believe in yourself and everything will be fine
Sincerely, A Black Man!

See with Your Mind; Not with Your Eyes

Robert M. Brandy

Opened up my 3rd eye
And I awoke in the 7th Heaven
Resurrected
In this place Love was my weapon
And poor people's needs were met and not neglected
Unity
We were all headed in one direction
And when God spoke to his people it was One message
And we listened
Freedom and Equality is what we were gifted
And Justice was on an everlasting mission with one Vision
Opportunities were everywhere because Poverty was missing
And when Hope spoke to her people she had everyone's attention
But the masses didn't believe in her until they saw Faith in the distance
To he who has an ear to hear then maybe he should listen
Too busy warring with each other over politics and religion
The youth are crying out for help
Take the time to listen.

Four More Years

Robert M. Brandy

In 48 months, truth will no longer be prolonged
For in these United States a child will be considered grown
My hands feel tied, nothing I say makes sense
When you're in a war with Poverty I guess only the dollars make cents
I'm like a penny with a hole in it
I have not to give
But words of enlightenment, jewels to pass to my kids
Four more years…
And I ain't talkin' 'bout no damn election
My son, my eldest boy will enter the world with no directions
No do-over's in life my friend, your choices will reflect your home
I just wish I was there to stand by you
So you wouldn't have to go through this all alone
Can't teach you to be a soldier in the middle of a war
Just strive for Greatness and remember who you are
Can't soar with eagles when you're running with snakes
Learn to embrace your struggles, you'll make some mistakes
This is from a father to a son, I know you'll do great
Just four more years
I can hardly wait!

The
Power

I Should Have Took That Plea (Spoken Word)

Robert M. Brandy

They Robbin' us Blind
We polluting our Minds
A second of Time
Could cost you a Dime
Stagnated for centuries
They stealing our Prime
Targeting our Youth
They takin' our Shine

Yes, VIRGINIA!
But what about them lynchings in Ohio
Where Niggas die slow
And kill quick for survival
Enslave your body by force
The Justice System is the only discord
So while we forced to believe that when we shoot in our appeals and our
    briefs
That the System GIVE A FUCK
NIGGA PLEASE
You better roll up ya sleeves
Got niggas emotionally scarred
From coppin' them pleas
Shit,
I could of been out in fifteen
(Damn)
I should have took that plea
Yeah, I know it sound crazy
But I should have took that plea
But my stubborn black ass couldn't get past
That this nigga took my bag
It was only a little bit of dope,
I could of let that pass

Now I'm sitting in a cell (pause) 14½ years done passed
I should have took that plea
But I felt that I was right and he was wrong
Now, see it happened at my home
I was 21 years of age
But hardly was I grown
If I would of took that 15 years
I'd have 6 months till I was home
Peace

Lost Parables

Cecil Johnson

If a friend compromises your worth, he sold you
Like chocolate stains on silk, they show through
Warriors tend to walk alone, that holds truth
Embrace every lesson in life, they mold you
Hate lingers with the eyes, you can't hide it
Don't completely trust idle minds, they're un-guided
Three may be separated, but not divided
Be conscious of the stories you hear, they're one-sided
How could we ever steal home, with no bases
Prison is our rite of passage, of all places
We persist to play with short decks, there's no aces
The Kings wear backwards smiles, with no faces
Regardless I'm in it to win, no small stakes
Conscious of the fangs and venom, from all snakes
Would you mix diamonds and glass? They're all fakes
No matter if it's sticks or bricks, it all breaks
Life is like steel on bone, a hard grind
Like a diamond left all alone, I still shine
Friendships are bridges of life, no small minds
Sistas are the essence of earth, no small dimes
Love is like the blessing of life, they're both sacred
Truth is like the seed from a womb, they're both naked
When flesh and soul separates, you can't fake it
Death is the answer to life, you can't shake it
Children lost respect for their names at what cost
The moment we reflected the same, our souls crossed
Venom circulates through veins like night frost, the stars
    never entered the game
We all lost

Will We Ever Be Equal (Spoken Word)

Robert M. Brandy

Why take from Me?
As if the system wasn't already gettin' over
And race had been a beautiful thing
Until the –isms came struttin' over
They say you can bloom wherever you planted
And while the rich get educated
I guess the poor gotta' learn to take nothin' for granted
But a wise man told me this
He said "Time the biggest snitch in the world"
And that you can have all the riches just don't worship the world
Whatever happened to the 8 months and 14 days
They can raise the price of gas
But not the minimum wage?
The way they giving out this time, yea we in the last days
And I guess Tupac had it right (yup)
Some things never change
Yet, we stay hoping for a change
Like the Man gon' give us Change
It's us against them y'all, we need to use our brains
Free my mind to lose these chains
Got me visualizing Dr. King and them
And all the sacrifices made
The Resolution is the Revolution
Ain't no disputin'
Tired of slave like mentalities being recycled through institutions
So what you got a higher education
And you got a decent job
Instead of emulating for the People you rather see us starve
You ain't even an Uncle Tom
For at least he helped free the slaves
But you too blind to understand that you just being played
The premonition of my strife became the premise of my life

Looking through my rear view I knew that prison was in sight
Was I a part of the three-fourths of angels that fall
Because now I dwell in a cell and it's hotter than Hell
And I'm still tryna find my way back home
Lost, trying to rationalize
My thinking saying "I don't belong"
Because where I'm from old ladies play numbers and hope they lottery hits
Young cats play ball and hope they lottery picks
Didn't need to stand trial
I was convicted in the womb
In a concrete jungle even a flower blooms
The Bible even says that the fastest don't win the race
And you can tell we near the end when God's calling all the Greats
We just lost Dr. Maya Angelou, did you hear the Heavens shake
And if my growth depends on freedom
Then what about my faith now brother
Damn that man who claims you 3/5 of a man
He only did that so we a never understand the strength of our clan
I stand unmoved when I say that I move for the People
Just cause our President was black, y'all, don't mean that we equal
Peace

Amurdica (Spoken Word)

Abu P. Crowder, aka "Spittin' Image"

How do you define terrorism?
Does anybody with a kufi or quotes the Quran fit this description?
By you puttin' your boots on the ground, is this your act of heroism?
In the name of propaganda and patriotism
You fight, you die, and you never question why
Ask yourself who owns the planes and who's quick to use the blame game
America!   America!   Amurdica!
Why aren't you invited to a briefing in the war room?
What's so secretive?
How come your soldiers get spoon-fed watered-down information?
A hero story is then conjured up and when you die you're coined a patriot
A die hard American would label me un–American
Because of my views on a condemned nation
Why? Because my naivete isn't such
I let you pretend to think you are slick
You are not by far!
I don't have to acknowledge the nosey neighbor to know she's watching
Her conflict resolution tactics are to divide and profit
Ostracize and conquer
With illusions and broken promises
How can a coward be dominant let's be honest
Why are you so astounded, you should be let down
Because the true terrorist is this America and their gung ho Americans
Democrats, Republicans and Libertarians
Under the same banner of an unjust government
Is illuminatis covenant
I fear for every black man, woman and child if domestic terrorism
    isn't addressed
Kill them instead of placing them under arrest!
When a traffic stop equates to death!
Ask yourself who's really foul
50 stars, 13 stripes, 7 red, 6 white

All from the labor of a colored man's plight
Damnn, we should be entitled to more
But you still consider me ⅗ of a man
You also try to glamour me with an "Impromptu Fantasy"
Of the American dream... Bitch Please!

Hopeless (Spoken Word)

Robert M. Brandy

I live in a world within a world
Dig this can you follow that
Forget about your wealth and notoriety
Can you bring my lil brother back?
And if that's your word why you don't honor that
I guess these walls just that tall, because I ain't seen my daughter yet
Acknowledge that
When you get up on yo podium
Sentence my man like he killed someone and he was only peddling opium
They selling dreams
He selling dope to some
And I know it's hard for us to believe sometimes so I'm guessing that's
    what hope is for
When the prisons got an open door
We all know who they searching for
They say education is the way out
My sister got a master's degree
And still can't find her way out
Hopeless…

Standard or Epidemic (Spoken Word)

Robert M. Brandy

Is it because of my approach that I speak the truth on purpose
While most of y'all believe in lies
I'm searching under the surface
Now that my dreams being postponed and restricted
I figured I'd take the time to deliver this missive
Then maybe you can depict it
Went from a shy kid, with dreams and ambitions
To a young black man finding his freedom in prison
Ain't too many options when yo skin isn't privileged
Open your eyes, and with your heart you should listen
I'm seeing way too many stars walk the yard of a prison
Now the question I want to ask you:
Is it just a Standard or is it an Epidemic?

Black History

Robert M. Brandy

No Justice, No Peace
Who police the police
When the system work against ya
Tell me how ya supposed to eat
Shot down Mike Brown
Left 'em dead in the streets
For the bread and the butter
They a treat us like some meat
Package us up
Put numbers on us
And ship us back out like packages brah
I love my black people
We just stuck in our ways
Gotta tell my ego quit
Get in the cage
Gotta teach the youngsters love
They full of that hate
Tired of eating from the crumbs
That fell off the plate
When you're a descendant of a King
Then ya destiny's great
They rather lock us up in cages
Planet of the Apes
Dawn of a New Breed
It's the Revolution
They tryna kill my whole clan
What's the solution?

Dedicate (Spoken Word)

Free Thought

Police kick in doors with deadly intentions,
And warrants to search for dirt and worse is the murder ending.
Now what's our response to our collapsed spirits,
If any it should be considered justifiably wicked.
When we cross us it's automatic killings,
But we adjust to what's unjust like we powerful victims.
Hopeless against the soulless, no focus and barely living,
I know, without vengeance it's hard to start repenting.
So y'all can feel us let's trade places.
After we kidnap ya, we'll take you to Africa.
On ships in compartments as small as a phone booth,
Then when we get there we trade you for fruit.
Force you to work for free and never feed you enough,
Tie you down, string you up.
We stereotype you on tv,
As products of incest with the potential to kill yo own family.
Rich junkies and the greatest liars and thieves,
Then we kill yo country
With a disease we create in a laboratory,
Separate, miseducate, and eliminate your identity.
Once you have nothing but suffering tears,
Then we dedicate you one month for four hundred years.

Tangible Strength

Dakota Flagg

"In order to paint a picture of freedom, we must first showcase the
canvas of circumscription!"

In therapy, they tell you to chase facts
Open your mind until you can rewind the dates back
Okay, so I was born in '92, Cleveland Ohio crack was hitting hard,
But my mother was hitting it harder,
Neglecting her 2 sons and only daughter
It's sad when you have a dad, but have to ask where he's at?
Even still we didn't know life was bad until he came back,
But I'll skip that.

8 years old with a cross to bare
By 11 I visited 3 group homes and 5 houses in a broken place called
    foster care
Sadly, nobody care about a little nigger's tears
As long as that check is running, nobody hears
Just the Lab Rats in this experiment while the "scientists" are working
their gears.

I'm 12 and a quarter now,
I'm my only supporter now,
In a new home with a lock on the refrigerator,
Constantly ridiculed by my captors, my fear is getting greater!
For amusement a room full of people tell you what you already know,
Like how your mother was a dope fiend and your daddy let you go,
You up to go, but they ain't having it, they tie you to a chair then they
    slam their fist,
Finally, they stop, they've abused too much,
Looking in the mirror with my face bruised up,
Thinking of a better life, I ran away,
Transforming into a Man from a boy in a night and a day,

12 and a half and I haven't even spoken the half,
I went and found my father, tried to barter for a place to stay,
But he ain't want to be bothered,
It just opened my eyes,
He's a product of this same experiment by which I'm victimized,
So I'm roaming the streets, nowhere to sleep but park benches and bandos'
I'm going bananas,
I'm cold and hungry with just the clothes on my back, and this black
   bandanna
Finally, the elements of the lab hits you,
"you got a fully loaded gun; think of what this will get you"
In my mind I wasn't a bad guy,
I'm just out there robbing the bad guys,
All them niggas who sold dope to my mother… yeah, they were in trouble.

I'm 13 with an apartment off Crehore
I left my city to get busy when they said I couldn't be more,
I'm good now, no lock on the fridge now
I'm 14, I got wifey and a kid,
Just another variable in they equation,
Back to the loaded clip/black mask; I'm on trash now,
As they predicted,
It goes quick from being 14 with a better life than you're living,
To 15 and serving life in prison.

You still don't get it?
Just because you've never seen the Bars it doesn't mean you aren't in prison,
The courtroom is an extension to the Laboratory; this isn't nothing different,
Unlimited funding for this experiment at the end of that gavel,
This is Wonderland, we're Alice lured by that rabbit – look how far
   we traveled,
True enough I am Frankenstein, this is how y'all made me,
If ya'll are the doctors who will save me?
But I get it
You put the one in Boxes,

And it irks you when you have his body, but his mind you can't lock it,
You fear the one who makes something when you gave him nothing,
Fuck You!

I refuse to be a product in yo test tube,
You said even as a first time child offender
I'm just a public menace; a lifetime re-offender,
Why? Because I'm young, Black, and a mental contender,
I figured you out; I see you in cloak and dagger,
No longer the subject; rather I'm the Master!
You said un-savable at 15, but I laugh at you,
I needed saving when I was abused, I'm no longer asking you.

Don't you see the mannerisms when I speak,
With the amount of respect that I gloat?
Polish, that's key; even when they said I was wrong,
I proved them dead wrong,
You made me then named me a criminal and a thug,
But refuse to show the public the true him,
That young child is human,
Put in an environment and survived!
If that's not Human Nature…they lied,
Even with this life y'all gave me I still ain't bitter,
Even though I'm so kind hearted,
Y'all find a way to paint a picture of a broken, cold-hearted nigger,
But the public isn't hearing it,
Because it's folks like us exposing this GARBAGE CAN EXPERIMENT!

New Day Pledge

Jason Hayes

I pledge allegiance to the one world order of disorder
To reorder the tribes of tribulation of this Nation
Who show no liberty or justice at all
And to the Republicans who work for the upper-class men against the
    Demo-crack-addictians
Who they feel have no morals at all
For the pros of congress making decisions to up their standards of living
When 99% of society is struggling to make a living
And the 1% that got it just ain't giving
Into the occupation of occupying Wall Street
So Brown Bears and Gold Bulls control the economy
For the lobbyists who are lobbying
Making back-room deals
Flipping coins to see which country to kill
For neighborhood watch men picking out which lil' black kid to kill
In the name of Justice or is it Just Us
For the banks bailing out on America
For the Bush era creating homeland terror
Then using the fear of the people to promote the War on Terror
Known as the war of oil on other countries' soil
For promotion of propaganda to sell props to consumers to garner the
    American dream
To those sitting on the Hill of the Capitol capitalizing off of America's Dream
To profiting off the pitfalls of the common man
To looking down on those who look up to Uncle Sam for a helping hand
To the constitution not being constituted
To police forces not being held accountable for whoever they shooting
To being more concerned with the Hunger Games
Than kids who go to sleep at night having hunger pains
To that ship that sailed before the Mayflower filled up with Africans
To the land that was promised without deed in hand
To the Free World of the Slave Master in a Racist America

So I pledge allegiance to Reorder the Disorder for the Tribes of Tribulations
    of this Nation without hesitation even if we must rot
There shall be Liberty and Justice for All…

Today is a New Day!

Contentment and Thangs' (Spoken Word)

Robert M. Brandy

Why is there division?
Because it's People who benefit
From yours and my division
We the commodity
So they build all these prisons
Lock us in cages
Why ain't we payin' ATTENTION?
100 years for a robbery?
That's a modern-day lynching
When Malcolm was speaking
Why wouldn't we listen?
Contentment and Thangs'

Ain't a black man allowed to Dream
Or will he become another example of what they did to Dr. King
They can trap our bodies
But a never kill the dream
Turn a young soul old
Oh, they a clip ya wings
We condition our minds to grind
Squandering years of our lives to crime
As if we were blind
Man, fuck them cops
It wasn't a crisis in America
When Philando and Alton Sterling got shot
Damn, this country full of hate
Why we imprison a prism in a country that supposed to be
SO FUCKING GREAT!
Contentment and Thangs'

I still can't breathe...
Politicians claiming that it's gettin' better

That's what they want us to believe
WE VOTE!
An exchange for a change
While the rich gettin' rich
The poor get short-changed
A damn shame
But won't a damn thang change
Cause we content
Peace!

Solidarity United (Spoken Word)

Robert M. Brandy

Solidarity United
United we stand, divided we fall
Sitting stationary, I watch the nation dissolve
Now we all gotta problem to solve

Sturdy like Buildings
Knowledge and Building
Black Men languish in prisons
What about children?
Who are raised in fatherless homes
Only fourteen, but act like he grown
Say he gotta be the Man of the house
Cause his Daddy ain't home

Seek and ye find
Destroy and rebuild
It's like for every kid that make it
Why a hundred get killed
My people ain't lost
Their visions misplaced
They see that we strive and tell us to wait
We know that love comes natural
Why they teach us to hate
Pissed off cause white cops kill black man
When the number one cause of death of my people
Is at the hands of a black man

We marching in the Chi just to keep the schools open
Whatever happened to that man's Dream
If Sky's the Limit
Why we down here on our damn knees
Amongst all of this ruckus

Why my people still suffering
Screaming no peace; We demand some justice
Man, it's deeper than race relations
Embedded in greed, drowning in hatred

Solidarity United
United we stand, divided we fall
Sitting stationary, I watch the nation dissolve
Now we all gotta problem to solve

If I'm into Pan Africanism
Why I call you my nigga
And they calling us niggas
Man, they treat us like slaves
Feed us like slaves
Even breed us like slaves
Most of us Kings, but we don't know it yet
All the potential in the world, but he ain't showed it yet
Say he on his grizzley
On his square 360
His kids they be asking about him
They say they miss 'em
In the belly walking upright and correct

And the State gettin' 36 thousand a year
Now that's a check
And his life no longer matter to them
It's a check
We a slave in the law books y'all
You betta check

Solidarity United
United we stand, divided we fall
Sitting stationary, I watch the nation dissolve
Now we all gotta problem to solve

Strong rule the weak
Wise rule the strong
Think she know everything
She ain't never wrong
If I was out there too I'd sing the same song
Jail cell the tomb
Classroom the cell
Both hands on the bible, I a never tell
A good book and a stick
Make sure my letter mailed

Solidarity United
United we stand, divided we fall
Sitting stationary, I watch the nation dissolve
Now we all gotta problem to solve

5 Minutes with the World

Major Cecil McCormick aka Magic

If I had five minutes with the world
The world would be mine in five minutes
I would have the whole world in my fingertips.

The gravity of every situation held in the palms of my hands weighed for
    clarity
Then printed out the lessons each one taught
And call it a book of pain
Then I'll explain
What is it to gain the world and lose your soul?

I had it all before the fall like spring and summer
I kept thinking the police couldn't get no dumber
I wouldn't sleep, couldn't slumber
I put in numbers and stayed underground with the plumbing
No identification no summons
Jewels, cars, clothes, shoes to shine, ride, and out-dress the rest
While I stumped and broke all the rules
I was cool – alcohol, drugs, women, you hear me?
The name of the game was elevating your chain
And hearing foreign chicks trying to say your name.

Yea I'm flying coach straight to the player's ball
With a coach that hate watching his players fall
Yaw yaw just don't understand, I was the devil's right-hand man
All types of nice, all types of scams
In all types of nights, with all type of plans.

We can go here, we can go there
A fair share of everywhere
Champagne, condos, express lanes, and lots of toast
But everything that glitters not gold

Chardonnay good, nice and cold
Another bunk and another story being told:

"Man I had it all before the fall like spring and summer
I kept thinking the police couldn't get no dumber
But they sent me sweet meat
She drove a hummer, in seconds we exchanged numbers
Now I'm doing a number like a lottery
But I've never hit a woman
When I got that summons I couldn't hear the music, my heart started
   drumming.
I couldn't believe he would set me up, an old detective."

Satan, he's very selective
A shrewd businessman in the evening
He's leaving his new place with a new face and a suitcase in the morning
He's tied up the night with all that excites
In the afternoon he sends all of his invites
24 hours, no rest, enticed to roll the dice
You sacrificed your life – dead end!
Until you accept Christ, believe me I know
because after the Devil stole mines
I had to get a new life.

Only a
Cage

Restless

Tony Curtis, Jr.

Living this life alone, memories of the past
Visions of the future
As I walk through the present surrounded by barbed wire and concrete
Dark souls all around me
Empty thoughts followed by anger
Heavy-hearted, no one understands this pain
Nobody else feels this hurt
This shit serious, no time for games
I'm at war with myself so I keep losing
Borderline insane, because every day is the same
True Insanity
Hoping to find a true friend, but how can they be?
When the truth they can't stand to see
Love, I forgot what that be
Misery, I can't forget that see
That's the only thing that won't leave me
If I told you what I seen, you won't believe me
Giving up, that's way too easy
Trust no one, people too skeezy
When a black man murder a black man
That's the real treason
Hated by my own kind, tell me what's the reason?
Refusing to Fall, I hate that season
Waiting for the Winter
I'm tired of losing
No alarm needed, I'm fed up with snoozin'
Wide awake
I see this shit for what it is
Got no children, but I'm still searching for fruit to feed the kids
So they ain't got to grow up in poverty
And see the same shit I did.

Four Nineteen

Robert M. Brandy

I'm hidden underneath mountains of insecurities,
Underneath there lies a blank canvas full of opportunities to explore,
Stripped down to my true essence; for I am afraid of the unknown,
So I cling to HOPE...
I'm learning to love me!

The lawn is littered with possibilities.
Dreams collect dust and rust then fall into the cracks and recede,
Paint peeling, broken windows adopt my physical frame,
I close the blinds when I'm inside so nobody else can see my pain,
Most people can't relate but to me I'm being safe,
City ordinances label me condemned,
Four walls pretend to be my friends,
They protect me from the elements, but they keep on holding me in,
But, the truth is I'm comfortable...
Gotta protect my intellectual property so I put locks on all the doors;
Couldn't trust my own thoughts so I put bars on all the windows,
And secured my back door with two-by-fours,
I admit my condition is self-imposed
A prisoner of my own mind – that's me...

Untitled

Siksteen

I wish I had not one wing but two
So I can fly away
North, South, East and West like Kanye
Touch the Sky is what I plan to do
Outside the exosphere a sign reading exit here, float on through
I testify I've been tested I see what I must do
Upon the request from my experience at a Bird's Eye View
From Jail Bird to Eagle past these gates I'ma soar on through
Overall, it's best to know I've learned that I can fly
I'm Celestial

Take Me to the King (Spoken Word)

Robert M. Brandy

She must see me with a crown
Not a frown
When she smile (pause) .
I just smile
Then My Spirit! ... Has to Rise Up from the ground
To the Earth (pause)
I still make my Momma proud
WOW (astonished)
Momma why I wasn't... the Chosen Child (pause)
Our Dearly departed was a Target
But, don't worry
He in Glory now!
Damn, (pause) I still make my Momma proud!
Like the day She seen me in that Gown
On that stage
Yeah, her smile was a smile
That had shined through the Crowd Man, I still make my Momma proud

Take me to the King
I'ah kiss His feet
This is way 'betta than
When 'Bron got them rings
And Karma come in 3's
She stubborn cause I'm stubborn
So I gotta deal with Me

My soul sings
But my Heart cries
Cause I done lost some things
Ok, I gave 'em up freely (sarcastic)
Now I know how Kunta felt (authority)

And why Frederick was reading all them damn books off
   that shelf (Tone swagg)
The only way to get Help

You 'gotta catch 'em with your other hand
Damn, I miss my "Brother Man"
That's why I'm yelling "FREE ME"
Or take Me to The King!

Sunshine Rosado

Robert M. Brandy

What is Death, but Life's unquestionable journey
Written in eternal ink, and sealed by the Heavens
Lonesome souls traveling upon the Earth
Patiently awaiting their day of rest.

He who knows ALL things question Him not
Though our pain exceeds our mortal bodies
His strength is everlasting
I will cry like the rain until the sun shines
I will sing like the birds for His love endures forever
Let us be content; for He is LOVE!

Nostalgia: A Longing for Something That Has Passed and Cannot Be Returned

Robert M. Brandy

Invest your time now
For tomorrow may not come
As a widow longs for her husband's warm embrace
My soul cries for forgiveness
Many nights I've questioned Life
If it's even worth living
He could have been anything in life
Instead he sits in prison
With enough time to die two-times
Before he finish his sentence
It's all Nostalgia to me
Like my mom who say she gonna stop
But keep on smoking
You can find truth
Even when a lie is present
Time is one's investment
And the future is our Blessing!

Freedom (Spoken Word)

Robert M. Brandy

Teachers "teach us"
Lead us
Where's our Leaders
Infants, youngsters, juvenile delinquents need us
Who else gon' carry the torch,
And open up the doors of Freedom
Yeah, you right
Our children need us
Learn your history
Knowledge is Freedom
Our Ancestors are watching over us
I know because I see 'em
The ground on which I stand is rising
And the truth will set a bound man free
But only if we listen
Instead we hear
Dismantling our hopes and our dreams
Because we here
Don't give up on your future my Brother
Because Freedom is almost near

Passage of Hope

Robert M. Brandy, Darryl Byrd & Tony Curtis, Jr.

How can a rose grow
At the bottom of a well
Who knew these seeds would blossom
Within the darkness when they fell
They were dropped in this pit
Because nobody saw their worth
But when they reached the bottom
Their foundation was planted in the Earth
They cracked out from their seeds
And then developed roots
They headed towards the light at the top
To find the truth
Some made it, some didn't
Some got tangled with the weeds
Thinking they would never grow
From being poor discarded seeds
But others met the bees
The bees were inspiration
And helped the roses to believe
The more they worked with one another
The more they could achieve
To never give up hope in life
Was a message from the bees
Confined within a darkened place
The roses still were free
A rose is still a rose
Even at the bottom of a well
Although we face adversity
Our Spirit will prevail

Today

Robert M. Brandy

Today I won't take for granted
That I awoke alive and well
My spirit is no longer held captive
I'll rejoice in my cell!

Today I won't be bitter and live my life with any regrets
I've been running from God for far too long
Today I'm going to rest
Today I'm a do something different to make a difference
Tired of just surviving and existing
Today I'm a make a change; take a stand!
Today, I'm trusting in God
Not in Man

Today
Today is a by-product of possibilities
Not yet known to the man who walketh with his head down
Defeated by life he left early and missed his blessing
Trying to do it all alone forced him to believe in something greater than
    himself
And that no man is an island

You can never get to tomorrow
Because soon as it happens it's today
For tomorrow never comes anyway
But there'll always be
Today!

Midnight Double Five

Robert M. Brandy

How can I be so close
Yet feel so far away
Been locked down 12 and ½ years
And it feels like just a day
God is on my side
I know, because when I got up off my knees
I looked out my window and there I saw a sign
Understanding is in your feet
They are up under you and they help you stand
And those will be the same feet
That will lead you to the promised land
It's Midnight Double Five
The time is soon to come
When all of God's creation
Will come together and be One!

I cry for help not knowing
If my tears will reach the masses
Even when my thoughts betray me
My actions stand unmoved
I fight against an unjust system
When the real war is with self
Tired of just existing
It's time for me to live!
Can't repay evil for good, because it cost too much to give
Time is on my side
It just hurts too much to wait
I have Strength; Courage; Hope; Patience
Now all I need is Faith!

A Message to All Women Around the World

Tony Curtis, Jr.

Understand that you are beautiful.

I know that you are worth the world, without you man can and will not exist.

Can't any man dictate what defines you no matter what he may make you
feel like.

Don't let him alter you in no way unless it is for the better and the growth
of you and him.

He must also practice what he preaches, hold him to the highest expectations,

Don't settle for less than loyalty, respect and love out of a man.

If he can't take you for you, he doesn't deserve you.

If he doesn't adore you with all your flaws, he doesn't deserve you.

If he can't treat you as the queen you are then don't waste your time.

You need no man to be strong, to be smart, to be confident,

To know you're beautiful or to know your worth.

You're the most precious of all the higher powers creations.

Heaven Spelled Backwards

Robert M. Brandy
Dedicated to Nevaeh Brandy

Water searches through streams
Bouncing off of channels
Moving in one direction with one destination
And that's to reach the Ocean

A seed has to die to grow
As a man has to die to live
Nothing ever stays the same
For life is just a constant flow

He spoke through Nevaeh
And it sounded like Heaven from the peace in her voice
Which reminded him that some good could come out of a tragedy
Life has but one face
Yet we seem to blame her for the suffering and all the casualties that obscure
   her path
While her true purpose was to be enjoyed
For her justice is fair in the eyes of the overcomer
But of great consequence to the faint at heart

Paralyzed by captivity
If only he could face his fears and fly
He'd find his freedom in the midnight hours
In those hours when everyone else was asleep
A still voice would echo loud enough for only him to hear
The voice gave him chills
And awoke him every night at the same time in a frightful state
Oh, how he'd wish that he could go into his cocoon
And hide away for those years of tribulation
And come again as a butterfly fully developed
He would fly away

Even if the lovely bird would loan him her wings
Maybe he could fly far away from his troubles into the land of the free

For in a moment's time, his knees buckled
And sweat beat down the middle of his strong back
It was then that he realized that "Freedom" was not a physical place
For she was even more desirous than what he imagined
And agreed to meet him right where he was at
But only under one condition
He had to take the first step
And in that step it signified a new beginning for him
For his life was forever changed
He was no longer held by bondage, by fear —
For he was free on the inside

The Girl of My Dreams

Robert M. Brandy

I'm growing fond of Her each day
When I'm in Her presence I get nervous
She challenges me to be my best without ever saying a word
She is strong, and yet so graceful
Her smile is light enough to brighten up my darkened day
I want to kiss Her lips or at the very least hold Her hand
But within this space there are boundaries,
And only so much a man can do
So, I must be careful to protect that which is sacred
A Bird and A Fish can fall in LOVE!
I wonder if She feels the same...

Nevaeh (Spoken Word)

Robert M. Brandy

She (pause) really gotta be strong
Cause she gotta grow up in this world all alone
Lost her grandpa to violence
Lost her daddy to violence
Now her Mom to the streets
Lost her life to that white shit
Now that (pause) that's really a crisis
Cause she ain't but 13 years old and already her life fixed
Got her questioning God
Asking where is this Christ at?
He turned water to wine
Can't He give this woman her life back
Instead she lay lifeless
And all the doctors in the world
Can't give this woman her life back
That's why she really gotta be strong
Cause she got a little brother and sister at home
In a year's time she lost her grandfather, her father
Now her mother is gone

She stood still with the breeze of the wind at her back
She was carrying a heavy load
Bearing the weight of the world
For nobody ever cut her no slack
And she knew that she was young
But how strong was her back?
And if she stumbled
She'd lose some things
But God gave her help with a mentality to conquer and achieve
She'd reach heights that only Heaven knows
I'm talking 'bout Nevaeh
That's why I say
She really gotta be strong.

Greatness

Robert M. Brandy

When I look at your face
I see a piece of me
You're like an angel sleeping on God's lap, having a peaceful dream
You can reach for the moon and touch the stars
But if you shall slip
The Angels will break your fall
Dust yourself off and strive to the end
When searching for Greatness
Look from Within

A Cage Is Only A Cage

Robert M. Brandy and Monica Fuhrmann

Will you think of me when the sky grows tired
And you rest your head?
Think of me,
The caged one said.

Will you not forget that you're the Gift,
More precious than rubies,
You move me.

It is I, myself, and Me!
Will you think of me?
The caged one said.

Spirit awakened patiently, waiting for my soul to be set free.
I am nothing,
The caged one said
But what about we?

We, said the bird, can be something
I will think of you when I fly through the sky
When I see the sun's rays breaking through the clouds
When I see the world in all of its complexity below me
Infinite, always moving
I will think of you and your soul will know
That one day we will be together
And we will be free!

Immortal

Robert M. Brandy

You got to understand death
So you can understand life
Though we feel the pain inside it's gon' be alright
I cried twice
I ain't talking about no tears of joy
The pain hurt from a loss
I'm trying to fill this void
You with Pops now and your memory is sacred
Death is the answer to life and we gon' make it

If August 6th a star was born
Why June 5th I got to mourn
You can live today and die tomorrow
T.Y. goodbye
Goodbye T.Y.

Yea we lost a hell of a man
If this is God's will, he got a hell of a plan
I'm telling you fam
The world gon' miss a hell of a man
Hit him too high give him some oxygen (damn)
Bring him back
Come on back
Come on back home
Don't you even care he got a daughter at home
I tried calling him twice he wouldn't pick up the phone
You already know Pops gon' welcome him home

If August 6th a star was born
Why June 5th I got to mourn
You can live today and die tomorrow
T.Y. goodbye
Goodbye T.Y.

I turned numb when I heard you was gone
Barely understood the other voice on the phone
All I could ask was, really, he gone?
I want to break down but I got to stay strong
I know you gone to your heavenly home
And your name I will carry it on
Can picture you now on your heavenly throne
Rest in peace T.Y.
You where you belong

If August 6th a star was born
Why June 5th I got to mourn
You can live today and die tomorrow
T.Y. goodbye
Goodbye T.Y.

Give Pops a hug for me. Tell him I miss him. You amongst Greatness now.
Don't worry about nothing down here I'm living for you now. You Immortal
and your name will live forever. I know death is just hiding you from us, but I
can still see you. Love you and miss you, keep shining.

A Letter to the Youth

Robert M. Brandy

My name is Robert Brandy, but everyone calls me Marlon. I've been in prison for the past 18 years. Prison is no place you want to be. This place is designed to kill your dreams.

Ask yourself this question and be honest with yourself when you answer it. What is holding me back from accomplishing my dreams? If we are honest with ourselves, the answer to that question is simple. You are! A lot of times we play a grave role in our own lives that lead us down the road of destruction. You are your worst enemy. We can't continue to allow our circumstances to postpone our dreams. It doesn't matter what you are going through. It will pass over just keep moving forward in spite of your obstacles. It doesn't matter if you come from a broken family with no father figures; if so, then you need to step up and be the man of the house and be the father you never had. It don't matter how many times you fall, just as long as you keep on getting up. So what if it takes you a little longer to accomplish your goals. What's important is that you accomplish them.

Today is the day that we make a decision on the course we want our lives to take. We have that choice! We can go down the road of destruction, chasing illusions such as selling drugs, joining gangs, and committing ourselves to a life of crime. Even though we know the end results to our actions, we still must understand that we have a choice because today is a choice.

It takes as much energy to dream small as it does to dream big! We can make that choice to chase after our dreams. One of the ways we do that is by creating options for ourselves. Staying in school and getting a good education is an option we create for ourselves. Staying away from drugs and gangs and placing yourself around people with similar goals creates another option for you. Remember this, you can do anything you put your mind to. Don't let anyone tell you that you can't. Nothing beats a failure, but a try. Opportunity knocks once, but temptation leans on the doorbell, so cease the moment. Today you have a choice, a choice to dream big!

Acknowledgments

I would like to thank God for giving me the courage to express my feelings with words and the strength to move forward in the midst of adversity.

My mom, Ann Benson, my sisters: Roberta, British, and Cherron. Thanks for believing in me and encouraging me with your support!

My brother David for encouraging me to write my very first short story: Pain, Perseverance, and Me. You believed in me when I didn't believe in myself.

Thanks to Monica Fuhrmann, without you this manuscript would not have found life! Thank you for your support and love!

Thanks to all the brothers who participated in the U.N.I.T.Y. program. Anthony Villa Sr. you taught me a lot in a few years that I will be forever grateful for! People for Change – Special thanks to Dr. Renee, Dr. Lynn, Dr. Elliot, and Susan! You guys brought to me the necessary education and tools I needed to refine my writing. Thanks for all the support and love! My final thanks is to all comrades behind jail cells and prison walls who continue to strive daily and defy the odds. Let us unite as one with one goal, FREEDOM!

In loving memory of:
Robert C. Brandy
Tyrone Brandy
Dorothy Law
Marry Mines
Elijah Paige
Ida Harrison
Monica Cool

About the Authors

Robert M. Brandy was born and raised in Youngstown, Ohio. A father of four children, he is a writer, poet, and the creator of U.N.I.T.Y. (Understanding Negative Influences Target Youth)—a program in which longterm offenders act as mentors to younger prisoners. The program's focus is on creating options, restoring hope, and teaching accountability. A proud member of the NAACP and Toastmasters, throughout his incarceration he has created or facilitated many programs geared to educate prisoners and create social change. Some of the programs include Breaking the Cycle of Mass Incarceration, Operation Growth, The Book Society, and Empowered Writing. As a University of Toledo student in the Inside/Out Prisoner Exchange program, he has written essays on poverty, religion, and prison reform. He is currently working on a screenplay and his autobiography, *Throes of Poverty*.

Darryll Byrd, A546610, is the author of a poetry book called *A Caged Byrd's Song,* which can be found on Amazon.

I was born **Abu Pharuq Muhammad Mustafa El Crowder**. I was blessed with a strong name so it was just a matter of time before I tapped into one of my gifts. I am a South Side native of Chicago (Englewood). I am 34 years old. I hope to inspire many to tap into their Godgiven abilities because words have power. I am a King and I now know my worth, and I continue to build my relationship with God and family. Time only has an effect on an idle mind.

Tony Curtis, Jr. was born and raised in Lima, Ohio. He is a poet, writer, barber, and artist. He is a co-creator of a traveling mural titled Passage of Hope that has been seen throughout Ohio. As a University of Toledo student through the Inside/Out Prisoner Exchange program, he has taken courses on race, gender, and politics. As a member of Toastmasters, he plans to use his voice and platform to bring attention to the injustices and discrimination that occur in the Prison Industrial Complex in hopes to end mass incarceration. While incarcerated he has been the facilitator of many programs including Operation Growth (a pre-G.E.D. program), Breaking the Cycle of Mass Incarceration, and Saving our Youth. He is currently working on a book of poetry along with art illustrations and seeking publication.

Dakota Flagg is 27 years old from Cleveland, Ohio. Raised in a broken system called foster care, I ran away from said system at the age of twelve, running away from abuse and neglect, running straight into the arms of the juvenile justice system at the age of 15 years old. Sentenced to 39 years to life as a first-time offender. But this does not define me. I am a father, a loyal friend, a poet, an artist, and a person…only if you knew me, you'd know this to be truth. God bless, contact me on jpay.com Dakota Flagg, 563937.

All the unchecked racism, injustice, and unfairness that happens to black people in this country has not changed—why? Is it because as soon as a black man or woman becomes a judge, prosecutor, lawyer, journalist, or gets any political job, they start acting and thinking just like the people they claim to be fighting? **Free Thought** is a published poet. His e-book, *Perfectly*, can be found on smashwords.com.

I'm **Jason Hayes**. I am a 37 year old that believes we as people need and should be aware of the true truth. I am a very aware and conscious person that is in tune with reality. We as people need to be unplugged from what some believe to be the matrix. I'm just a plain Jane guy seeking knowledge and understanding, who hopefully one day will make a real impact on today's society. The youth is the key to our success. Jason Hayes #475-407

Major Cecil McCormick is Choctaw Indian, Scottish, and African American. He is 46 years old and has written 12 books that he is in the process of publishing. He has lived in Hollywood, California, and dealt with the cast studios and managers, but chose to write his own path. He does open mic as well as writing all forms of poetry.

A Note from the Editor:
We were unable to obtain biographies from Cecil Johnson, Kevin Short, Siksteen, and Andre Winters by the time of publication.